The New Rules
Of Baseball Instruction

What every parent and player must understand

about playing at the next level

Paul Reddick

Table of Contents

This book is dedicated to all those who love
and play the game of baseball.

INTRODUCTION

My mission is, has, and always will be to take confusing and frustrating baseball information instruction and coaching and make I very simple for the average, everyday dad, coach and player. I want to work with the people that want to have a great career, want to make the most of their potential. They don't have ridiculous delusions of thinking that they're going to be the next Babe Ruth or the next Derek Jeter. Now, you may be the next Babe Ruth or the next Derek Jeter, and I hope you are. My goal is not to diminish your goals, but my goal is to get you to focus on the thing that will help you reach whatever goal in baseball that you have.

There are really two sides of the baseba
world. There's the confusing side and the fr

The confusing side is those esoteric educational coaches that are high up on their horse, they use words that are too big, they make things that are too complicated, you read their stuff, you watch their videos, and you don't even know if they're talking about baseball anymore, it's so complicated and confusing. Now, maybe they're well intentioned, but ultimately, their information is not readily accessible to the average everyday coach, player and dad who just wants to get better. Not only do you not have the time to understand that kind of instruction, let alone understand it, but actually apply it, use it, and then tweak and correct it as you go. There's that confusing side.

Then there's the frustrating side. That's what we call the "traditional baseball coach". They have their blurbs, their buzzwords, their sentence fragments and the things that they yell out at games. They all sound good when they yell them out at games, but they're not part of any kind of complete program or any kind of complete instructional theory or practice. That can be very frustrating when you are doing things the right way, but you're being taught the wrong things. Ultimately, you're being taught you're doing the wrong things right, and you wonder why we don't have the results.

Well, let me tell you something. I know something about you. If you have this book in your hands, there are a few things I know about you. Obviously, you read books and you'll invest. You're willing to take the time and to spend the money to get better information. Number 2: You've probably been to camps and clinics so you're willing to get out there and see other forms of information and other ways of coaching. You've probably done private lessons, so you're willing to invest in specific instruction to you at a much higher cost. You probably have DVD courses and other books, so there's no doubt that you're willing to invest, spend time, read, and seek out the best. But, aren't those the traits of a successful person? They are, so you have all the right behavior, but if you don't have the right results, you wouldn't be reading this book right now, if truth be told.

What follows is an interview between Harold Reynolds and I. I literally went to my friend, Harold Reynolds, who I know is the toughest interview in baseball, and I said, "Harold, don't let me get away with anything. Challenge me at every turn and if I don't make sense and if I don't sound like I'm telling the truth, I want you to call me out on it," and he did several times and we had a great discussion. What follows is the transcript of that discussion. I hope you'll enjoy it.

Please excuse any kind of grammatical errors or flow, because it wasn't dialogued and written like a book report. I know you'll get the message that comes through in this book, and we'd love to give you the free videos of this book. If you go to freebaseballvideos.com, you can get the free videos of this entire DVD. It was shot at the Yogi Berra

Museum and Learning Center where I am a camp director. It was an unbelievable afternoon. Like I said, Harold didn't let me get away with anything. He challenged me at every turn and what you're going to find in this book is an eye opening, and I hope career-changing omen for you.

I wish you the best. I wish that every baseball dream that you have becomes a reality. I hope you enjoy the game. I hope you grow closer as coach and player, player and parent, father and son, whatever your relationship is. That is my goal. I love this game, I love the people that play this game, and I want you to make the most out of your career. The best of luck and don't forget to get the free videos of this interview, Harold and I live at freebaseballvideos.com.

THE BASEBALL POTENTIAL TRAP

Reynolds: Let's talk today about Reddick Educational Center. We're going to talk about five major topics that can affect you as a fan, a parent, or even a kid who's watching, who's participating.

Number one is potential. We always hear, "Oh this kid's got the best potential going. He's got a chance to be so-and-so." So we'll see how you might be able to fulfill that potential.

Number two, we'll talk about development. How do you develop? What is development in baseball and how important is that?

Number three, coaching. Who's going to coach? Who knows what they're talking about? Who doesn't?

Who should we be listening to? Who shouldn't you be listening to? We'll get into coaching.

The fourth thing will be instruction. What is instruction? Is it stopping the game and being able to explain why you made a mistake, or is it just plowing through it, seeing who can hit the ball hardest to you, and seeing if you can catch it? We'll get into that and maybe help you fulfill all these things.

The last and final subject is the hot topic everyone's talking about, pitch counts. We're going to talk about pitch count all the way from Little League to the big leagues. Everybody has pitched, and a lot of kids are hurting their arms in Little League before they even get a chance to get started on our first topic, which is potential.

So, Paul, let's get into potential because it affects everybody in the game of baseball no matter what position you're playing—infielder, outfielder, pitcher, catcher, whatever. The word "potential" is thrown out a lot. What are your thoughts?

Reddick: It's a word that's constantly there. Especially at the younger ages, we hear, "That kid has a lot of potential," or even looking back on their career, "They had a lot of potential." I look at the word "potential," and what it really means is that something could be better.

Looking at a kid with a strong arm that strikes out 15 kids a game, we think he's got potential to develop that skill into playing at a higher level. Or we get the kid who's a little bigger and stronger and can hit home runs. But really when you break it down, there's a difference—there's a huge gap—between potential and potential realized. And in the middle of that gap, if you take someone's potential, their genetic gifts, and you match it up with the skills of the game, that's when you can really see potential realized.

Now that "skills of the game" middle part, it has a lot of pieces. It's got the X's and O's, obviously, mechanics and fielding, but there's also baseball intelligence, IQ—knowing the game and knowing how to play the game. Then there's training, conditioning, and mental aspects, all the things that go with being a player. We're missing that middle part.

I always go back to the Little League World Series. During that broadcast, there's more talk about potential than anything else you see on TV. We see this little 11- or 12-year-old kid striking out the best players at that age group, and we say, "How can these kids miss? In ten years we should see this kid in the big leagues." Right? But that's not happening. In fact, in the 70-plus years of the Little League World Series, I don't know how many players, but let's say 1,000 a year have gone to Williamsport. There are only 24 players from that group who have played in the big leagues.

Reynolds: Wow.

Reddick: Now if you think about it, if we took the best 6,000 11- and 12-year-old basketball players, well, we would've seen some superstars in there. You know, we're seeing that earlier and earlier, right? In other sports we see this. So what happens between that gap?

Reynolds: Yeah, why are they not fulfilling that potential?

Reddick: Why are they not? I always show this little cartoon. I think you'll like this. This is Dennis the Menace, right? He's in trouble, in the corner, and what he says to his parents is, "If you are raising me right, how come I get in so much trouble?" I would say to coaches, "If we're doing such a great job as coaches, why are more kids exiting this game than ever before?"

"If you're raisin' me right how come I get in so much trouble?"

We have more opportunity to practice the game; there are indoor facilities, which seem to be in every town. I don't know how many indoor facilities you practiced in when you were a kid, but I remember driving 45 minutes to go to a place that had a batting cage to hit for a couple rounds.

And then there's information. Anyone can log onto the Internet 24/7 and see the videos you have on baseball training, they can see the videos I have and get better. So why are we missing? We have more medical intervention than ever before. We know more about the arms.

Reynolds: You got me. Why are we missing?

Reddick: Let me back up a little bit, here.

Reynolds: Okay.

Reddick: There's also a problem in America with the way that we go for sports. Now, 50 percent of all minor leaguers are players from outside the country. And I think it's like 35 percent of big leaguers are players from out of the country. I served in the United States Coast Guard Auxiliary; I defend that freedom as much as any person to come here. America is the great melting pot. But we're missing something here in our development in America. No other sport has that percentage of players from other countries. Hockey is only like 18 percent of players from other countries. Basketball, even with the influx of...

Reynolds: This is supposed to be the American pastime.

Reddick: Right. Right. So with the influx of European players in basketball, it's still only like 18 or 19 percent of players outside the country. So we're missing something here, and it's radically changed over the last 10 to 15 years.

About 10 years ago I did a study published in Collegiate Baseball magazine. We looked at professional pitchers from 1961 and 2001, and it wasn't even close; the durability of the pitchers then, the innings pitched—and remember too that at that point, they were playing with almost half the competition and some four-man rotations. So it was very common during that time, the '40s, '50s, '60s, even into the '70s, that you would see the top ten pitchers in complete games have double-digit complete games.

In the last 13 years, only one pitcher has completed more than ten games in the big leagues. Now there's a lot to that, right? You know there's relief pitching and health and stuff like that. But with all that caring for the pitcher, we haven't seen any reduction in injuries. Injuries are up 300 percent, and in some age groups, up 700 percent. You know, you've heard the stories of kids getting operated on when they're 10, 11 years old.

Reynolds: Right. Tommy John surgery.

Reddick: Right.

Reynolds: At 10 and 11 years old.

Reddick: So there's that huge gap that we're missing in there.

And that's where we have to focus—on what happens when we notice potential versus the end game. Where do we end up from there?

Reynolds: That's interesting stuff. I think the one thing when I think about this potential and what's going on in the country is that we have a lot of kids playing other sports, too. So we don't allow them to fulfill their baseball potential because we're saying to pick a sport right now. Baseball's a game that you ...

Reddick: You have to play it year round.

Reynolds: Yeah.

Reddick: You play one sport year around.

Reynolds: Yes. And with baseball, it's going to take time to hone those skills that are so unique compared to other sports. Is that a problem, too?

Reddick: Yeah, we've talked before about the fact that there's more to being a kid and playing sports than just focusing—and it's probably the worst thing that you can do. You know, to play other sports, basketball, football, you have to be well rounded, and it also gives you the opportunity to compete in kind of different ways and develop other athletic abilities. Other sports require different skills and athletic abilities that we're not seeing developed; especially when the kids start to specialize or play year round.

There's a social aspect, too. Kids need to be kids. They need to be around other kids. It can't just be this bubble that we're raising them in. Even if it is baseball, I think it's a horrible thing.

I always tell kids when they go to high school, they say, "Well, I think I'm just going to stop playing football or basketball and just focus on baseball." And I say, "All right, you understand that you're never going to play football again for the rest of your life. This is it. You're retired."

You're not going to come back when you're 25 and go and decide you want to play a little football. So, you might as well enjoy this time where you can still participate in these activities and develop athletically and socially.

Reynolds: So in closing, when we think about potential, the other question is, are we over-projecting people? Maybe their potential isn't as great as we think it is.

Reddick: Yeah. Well, if you see a nine-year-old kid who shows a genetic gift—and we're going to talk about this later—we throw them into this blender of training and "elite" and all these words we throw at kids, and we never give them that room to breathe, room to grow.

Get 20% off any of the proven programs in our catalog.
There's something for players of all ages and skill levels.

www.PaulReddickBaseballVIP.com

Use coupon code: HAROLD

THE SCARY REALITY
OF COACHING TODAY

Reynolds: All right, we've talked about potential and development; let's discuss coaching. Paul, you have an extensive background in coaching. You've done camps, you've coached teams, you've coached in the minor leagues, and you've been around a lot of coaching. So the headline is coaching. Take it away.

Reddick: Well, I think today we've got a huge problem with unqualified coaches entering the game.

Reynolds: You're stepping on some toes already.

Reddick: Yeah, that's okay. I think back to the way I started coaching. I started as a volunteer assistant for a junior American Legion baseball team because that was the way you started in coaching. There was no place to go other than Little League or Babe Ruth League. But even then you still had to work your way in.

So I starting coaching under a guy named Jack Byrnes. I think we all have a coach that has that impact. Jack Byrnes is like a second father to me. Probably every good thing in my life has happened as a result of meeting him.

I was his volunteer assistant, and for one year I sat on the bench and he would talk to me about the game and he would talk to me about what you would say to one kid, how you can't coach every kid the same. This is what you do in this situation and this is why that. This is what you say to this kid when he makes an error. This is what you say to this kid when he strikes out. This is when you get on a kid and this is when you back off a kid, and this is how the footwork on a double play is taught and this is how you dive back to first on a pick off. Every little intricacy of the game he taught me.

And my second year I coached first base. My third year I coached third base and my fourth year I ran the whole junior Legion team. You know, that was a huge deal. He brought me along slowly and taught me the game.

Today there's no vetting process for getting in. You can just get in. If you've got the money and you've got the team together, you can get an affiliation with an organization and just go play. It's become very easy to "anoint" yourself in this game. Ten or 15 years ago or 20—more than 20 years ago when I started coaching—it wasn't like that.

The only way you could get to a position where you could coach a varsity team, for instance—and even after being with Jack, I spent two more years as a high school assistant and then I coached professionally. The only reason for that was I coached with a guy named Ray Korn who's a legend in New Jersey. He's coaching professionally and helped me on that path.

So I had these great mentors to teach me coaching. It's not there anymore. Now you can enter the game with no qualifications that you know how to coach, not even the qualifications of the game. You might have to take a safety course and stuff like that, basic courses.

It's a very dangerous situation when we have these people that enter the game and don't know anything about it. They know about baseball, but they don't know how to coach, and that's a totally different skill.

Reynolds: There's no way I could walk into IBM and go, "You know what? I've got an idea. Here's what we're going to do."

Reddick: Right.

Reynolds: But we do that in baseball. You know, I couldn't walk onto a NBA court and say, "You know what?

Larry Byrd, I know that you decided you wanted to be a general manager but you don't know what you're talking about. Here's what we're going to do."

Reddick: Right.

Reynolds: Because this is what I'm learning in a book. Right? I've read about it or whatever.

Reddick: Right.

Reynolds: We allow that to happen in baseball.

Reddick: Overwhelmingly allow it to happen.

Reynolds: And I'm on your path because I think it's hurting this generation of kids who aren't able to have that life experience where somebody's able to say, "I've lived this, young man. Trust me. This is how you do it."

Reddick: Right.

Reynolds: We're losing that.

Reddick: You know, Jack Byrnes, he's coached for 20 years. And he gave me that education.

We choose coaches on all the wrong criteria. This is an email I got from a guy who asked me about a kid that I knew.

He said, "I'm going to take my son here for instruction. What do you think?" And I said, "Well I don't know how good he is as a coach." And this guy and I emailed dialogue back and forth, and he said, "But he said he knew you." And I said, "Yeah, I do know him. I knew him when he was a player. And I don't know how he is as a coach, because being a great player and being a great coach are two radically different things." But when we pick instructors or we pick coaches to coach these teams, we tend to bring in people that had great playing careers.

One of the reasons the guy I was talking to was picking this guy for instruction was that he was the best player that ever came out of that area. But that doesn't qualify him as a coach.

Now of course there's an experiential factor that he can bring to this kid. But can you imagine if we only picked major league managers based on their playing career?

Reynolds: It'd be a shame.

Reddick: Yep. Because look at the three managers that retired recently: Tony La Russa, Bobby Cox, and Jim Leland. There's three of the top, would you say top ten managers of all time? They're certainly in the discussion, right? Their playing careers were a year or two in the major leagues.

Reynolds: Not even La Russa played more than 1 years' worth in the majors.

Reddick: Is that right?

Reynolds: Yeah.

Reddick: Okay. I didn't know that. So, when we think about it, we don't sit down and say, "Let's call up Mike Schmidt because he was the best player," or, "Let's call up Cal Ripken." Now they might make great managers, but predominantly our best managers have been players that really weren't that great. Even like Joe Girardi, Mike Scioscia, and Joe Torre, they had good careers but they weren't superstars of their time.

We select coaches based on the wrong criteria. We should be selecting coaches based on how good a coach they are. I tell players and parents when they're selecting a coach, "Don't look at how many 'nines' they coached because that's what a weak coach can do. They can surround themselves with nines and tens." And when someone enters the game as a coach with no qualifications, that's the biggest cover. That's the easiest way to cover yourself. If you don't have anything to teach or you don't have the skill, the ability to teach, just go get a bunch of great players. We all know the secret to coaching is talent, but there are those great coaches that are able to mold talent.

Our criteria should be not how many nines and tens they coach but how many fours did they make into sevens? How many sixes did they make into eights? Because that's where 90 percent, and maybe more, of all of our players are; they're fours, fives, and sixes, they're average.

Reynolds: So I'm a parent sitting on my couch right

now and I'm listening to you and I say, "I want to coach." What are some of the keys for me getting in, and what should I know about coaching?

Reddick: I think you have to get experience. Just like you said, baseball's a game that takes time to learn. And I think the best thing that you could do, at least for a year or two, is just go sit and volunteer with someone. Go find the most experienced coach. Go find that guy who is perpetually old, right? There's always one in every league. He's been coaching forever, and that's the guy you want to just sit down with and listen to. Talk about the game.

I had an opportunity one time to fly out to California to a coaches' convention. I happened to sit down next to a college coach on the plane. It was a six-hour flight and I asked him, "What do you think is the most important thing about coaching baseball?" He didn't stop. He didn't come up for air the whole flight. You know, it was a six-hour flight. He could've gone on for 12 hours.

You want to seek out those people who can really teach you not only about the X's and O's of the game—it's important; everybody knows that—but you also have to know how to deal with players and you have to know some players need a push and some players need a pull. Sometimes you need to form a more tightknit team. Some guys need a little extra work; some guys need to be screamed at every single day. There are all kinds of different things. So I think the thing that's been the greatest gift for me is to be kind of an apprentice. I think if you seek out those coaches, not only will you learn a ton, but you're also going to be really surprised at how open a lot of people are to talking about the game, to teaching you the game, and to passing that on. I think that's probably the most important thing.

THE NEW RULES
OF BASEBALL INSTRUCTION

Reynolds: All right, our fourth topic is instruction. This is a dicey one because it can go a lot of different ways when you start talking about instruction. Do what I say, not what I do, or maybe do what I'm always saying and don't think about anything else. You know, there's a lot of ways you can go on this and it can be a tough subject.

Reddick: Right.

Reynolds: I'm curious about your thoughts on instruction.

Reddick: Well I think Tom House said it best when he said that the biggest problem in baseball is bad information from credible sources. We talked about it before—because someone is a great player, we think that makes that person a good coach or a great teacher or someone that we can learn from. And there's a lot we can learn, tons that we can learn.

But I think there's a huge problem between what people hear and what actually happens. Even with professional players, I think this is probably our most argumentative segment here. And I've had this discussion with dozens of MLB players. But what I look for is what's objective, what's happening without any other preconceived notion or any other thought about it.

The term "conventional wisdom" means something that's been repeated over and over again for so long that we think it to be fact.

The most famous conventional wisdom theory is that the earth was flat. Everybody believed that because enough people said it. Then we learn objective information that the earth is round, obviously.

But that's the way it goes in baseball. We hear these buzz words, sentence fragments, these blurbs—they get flung around in the game, but there's no real cohesive or complete instructional program around them. We see a lot of stuff that just gets fired off. Coaches will yell stuff: "Bend your back, get your elbow up, follow through, snap it off, head down, elbow up, knees back"—whatever they're saying now, a hundred different things.

I have a few examples that we use in our instruction. When we talk about the bad information from credible sources I use these pictures. This is from Randy Johnson's book.

This is a picture of Randy Johnson demonstrating the proper release point, saying it's up here. So now if we're sitting in a room, and I'm there and Randy Johnson's there, who are you going to listen to?

Reynolds: I'm listening to Randy.

Reddick: Randy, right? Because of his 5,000 strikeouts or whatever it is. But the problem is that this is where Randy thinks he releases the ball. This the cover of the book that I wrote, and this is where he actually releases the ball. I don't know if he's out teaching this, but he's saying, "I release the ball up here," and then he goes to pitch and that's not what happens. So there's a genetic or an instinctual thing that he does when he pitches. He knows how to get it done.

Reynolds: I think it's funny because we're in this information age and we're thinking about how the earth was flat. Of course we ultimately realized it was round when we got more information about it. The same thing is true with video now; it gives you a lot more information. I remember | I got off to this tremendous hot streak one year in Seattle and I was like, "I've got my hands up here and I'm just raking them." I'm telling everybody because that's what I feel like in the batting cage. It's like, "I'm Dave Parker and I've got my hands up here." And all of a sudden I went home and I'm watching the news one night and they're showing me hitting and I've got my hands way down here. And I'm getting a base hit and I'm thinking, "Well that's not where I had my hands." And I realized that my feel is different from what I'm seeing. You know what I mean? I had a feel for it but it wasn't the same as the visual. I think a lot of times with players that's what happens because so often it's a feel thing. Here's what I feel like, and they'll say, "Get on top of the ball so you swing down." Well, you're not swinging down at the ball. Nobody's swinging down like this. You're swinging like this. So those are things that happen with players. Like Randy might think, "Get your hand up here," but he's actually throwing three-quarters.

Reddick: Right. Where did you think you threw?

Reynolds: I probably threw more side arm.

Reddick: Okay. It's interesting you bring up the hitting thing because we also use this—and this is from Don Mattingly's book, where Mattingly is thinking he is when he approaches the ball.

Now this is where he is when he approached the ball as a player.

You talk about swinging down, so this is where he thought he was at—where his arms snapped straight after contact, but this is where they really snap straight. There's a big disconnection between—if we pick up a book from Don Mattingly, we're going to listen to Don Mattingly, you know, because he's Don Mattingly.

Sports Illustrated wrote a very interesting article about what it really takes to hit and to be a great hitter. And they used Jennie Finch. Remember the softball player and how she used to go around on *This Week In Baseball*? Did she strike you out?

Reynolds: I never faced her.

Reddick: Oh, okay.

Reynolds: She struck out Bonds and all these other guys. I remember when she was going around doing that.

Reddick: And the argument was—it's going just as fast as they faced from a live pitcher in a game. But then they thought, "Well it's a shorter distance," and all that. But what it really boiled down to was information; that great hitters are great collectors of information and retrievers of information. So a 90-mile-an-hour fastball, or a 95, I think was the equivalent of Finch, coming at them from a normal pitcher's angle, they had information on that. But they didn't have as much information on one coming from down low. So over time they could collect enough information to retrieve it and to be able to react and hit.

That being said, that calls into question some of the most sacred hitting instructing tools—the tee, the soft toss, and these things that are staples, that some people swear by. But if being a good hitter is collecting data, we'd be better off always hitting that live pitch coming at us. Now I know there's psychological reasons why guys use the tee to calm down and stuff like that. But as far as skill development and hitting in a game, we're better off having our grandmother out there throwing like this than maybe hitting a ball off a soft toss.

Reynolds: From the mental development standpoint is what you're saying.

Reddick: Yeah. So we've seen players—Andrew Jones, I think, maybe is one of the best. He seemed to have a step on everybody. He was moving before the ball was hit. And Andre Agassi was like that. There was a picture we had of Andre Agassi where the ball was on the racket of the other server, and he was moving.

Reynolds: Moving in anticipation.

Reddick: Yes. But he collected information, data and information. We just have to think about our instruction, and video has helped, too. Video is as good as the person looking at it. So I did a lot of work early on three-dimensional motion analysis. We still do some of it. What I find is that a lot of people go to video wanting to confirm what they think is right and not looking at it and saying, "What's really happening here?" So if I'm on a roundtable with Don Mattingly and Randy Johnson, I'm not going to get a lot.

Reynolds: I think the other part of it though is that I don't think we'll ever figure out how it's done because each individual processes it differently. I remember Tony Gwynn, who very rarely swung and missed. I never swung and missed very much either. If I swung, I was going to make contact. And Tony would talk—I asked him, "Where do you pick up the ball at?" You know, some people say, "I look at the square here," and all that. And Tony would say, "Go from the bill of the cap, from the logo to here because I don't want my eyes to get lazy, and then I'd go there and I'd pick up the ball." Well I watched his whole arm and he started back here. I was watching the arm the whole way.

Reddick: Right.

Reynolds: And so ...

Reddick: I'm sure that would make another hitter maybe

...

Reynolds: Yeah, it would drive them crazy.

Reddick: Crazy, yeah.

Reynolds: So it comes down to what you can do. I also

heard, you know, the old timers—Willie Mays, Hank Aaron, and those guys, they would sit and the—let me see your hat real quick. They would take a hat and then the bead of the hat, and they would sit there and they'd watch the pitcher through the little hole and be able to eliminate all the other moves to be able to see things.

Reddick: Yeah.

Reynolds: Well I did that. It didn't help at all. So, you know, it comes down to what each individual can do. I don't know if we will ever get to the bottom of it.

Reddick: Well Yogi used to say that what helped him was hitting bottle caps with a broomstick ...

Reynolds: Yeah.

Reddick: ... when he was a kid—those things would go all over the place. At one of the coaching conventions about 15 to 20 years ago, a really famous hitter got up there and he had 35 minutes to talk. He got done with everything he knew about hitting in seven minutes and asked, "Who's got questions?" A guy goes, "How do you hit a curveball?" He was kind of like that (demonstrating swing).

But throw him a curveball and he'll hit it. And I think what you bring up when we talk about instruction is that we're not backing off enough to let you have your process, to let you be who you are as a hitter and to let you pick up where you want to pick up the ball. Before you played professionally, did you hit off a batting machine or hit off a tee?

Reynolds: Nothing. It was always thrown to me; the ball was always thrown. Maybe I started doing some flips as I got older, but for the most part they weren't pitching machines and all that stuff.

Reddick: So the question is, how has that improved us?

Reynolds: There was a hitting coach in San Diego when Tony Gwynn was putting up these big numbers all the time and I was fortunate to work with him one year. He said that every hitter would hit .400 if we didn't have any instructors.

Reddick: Yeah. Exactly.

Reynolds: Because everybody gives you something to think about.

Reddick: Yeah. You know, one of my favorite Yogi stories—I always prod him about what you guys do in spring training—"Tell me what you did"—and I always thought he didn't want to ... But you know, he said to me something one day and I never asked him again. He says, "Look, those who figured it out figured it out and those that didn't, didn't." And I thought, "Yeah, all right. Yeah, I got you, Yogi." You know, that makes perfect sense because they just let those guys play. So how have the numbers improved? Are the hitters better today than they were 30 to 40 years ago? Are the hitters better today than when you played? Maybe they trained a little bit ...

Reynolds: Trained more, a little stronger ...

Reddick: They're not better.

Reynolds: No, I don't think they're better.

Reddick: You can't tell me you couldn't put Rod Carew in today's game and he wouldn't still be Rod Carew. He'd be Rod Carew no matter what generation he plays in. So how did the hitting machine and the tee—where's the improvement?

You know, when we look at other areas of life, the Internet's made our life easier. It's a great invention. But none of those things happen in baseball. You know, where's the indoor facility? The travel team? Where's the impact?

In 1961, the players were much more durable against half the competition. I think it was 16 teams, I believe, then. So a little bit less than half the competition; much more durable, much more successful. With all the things we've come up with in instruction, where's the improvement? It's not there.

Reynolds: That's the question.

Reddick: Yeah.

Reynolds: Those who do, do, and those who don't, don't.

Reddick: That's right.

THE TRUTH ABOUT PITCH COUNTS

Reynolds: All right, our final subject is pitch counts. Now you think, "Paul, you've ruffled some feathers already." Sit back and listen to this conversation on pitch counts. Probably the most controversial thing in baseball is the pitch count.

Reddick: Yep. Of all the attention it's gotten over the last ten years—again, where's the impact? Where's the reduction of injuries? Where's the increase of production of the players? Where's the performance? It's not there.

There's no saying, "We're watching pitch counts and look what's happened because of that." I have a lot of admiration for Little League and for ASMI and the people that have tried to do something, but I have to disagree and I have to say that what they put out is flawed.

First of all, it's not about the number of pitches you throw. In the Little League rules, a nine year old can throw 65 pitches, a twelve year old can throw 75. So I don't know what's worse, that we only think a 12 year old can throw 75 or we think a nine year old can only throw 10 fewer than a 12 year old. That's a huge development gap between there.

It's never about the number of pitches that we throw, and I'll tell you why. I started off as an injury guy. That was my background as a pitching instructor, was helping kids who were injured get back on the field.

I worked with St. Barnabas, which is a big medical center here, Health South, and dozens of other places.

After the pitchers would get cleared, they would come and work with me for what we would call performance rehab. A kid would come in and his father would say, "My kid got overworked. He got abused; he threw too much, too many games, the whole story." But for every kid like that, I had a kid's father come in with the clipboards of his pitch count. His kid never threw more than 60 pitches in a game. He iced his arm. They rubbed goat's milk on his arm after every game and he slept in a hyperbaric chamber and he's hurt, too. He has the same injury as the kid whose arm got overused.

When it comes to pitch counts, we have to think of it not as the number, but how we arrive at the number. I can show you how a pitcher can very safely throw 105 pitches and be completely risk free and throw 55 pitches and be at risk for injury.

The first problem with the Little League model is that it makes a lot of assumptions. Now there's a lot of them, but I'll go into the major ones.

The first one is that we're assuming that everyone is equal, that they're coming to the game equal. So do we have a kid that's just come from a basketball game who's going to pitch, do we have a kid that just threw 50 pitches in the bullpen and is going to pitch versus a kid who threw 30 or 40 or warmed up properly and didn't abuse himself in the bullpen? That's one assumption.

The second assumption is we're assuming all pitchers are equal. Take a kid with good mechanics that throws 65 pitches, and then a kid with bad mechanics that throws 65 pitches—well that's going to be night and day. Now we have to agree on what's good mechanics. That's a whole other discussion. But that's another assumption.

The third assumption is that all pitches are equal. So a fastball thrown by Roger Clemens is going to be much more stressful on his body than, say, a fastball thrown by a Greg Maddux, Jamie Moyer, or Paul Byrd type of pitcher. So we're assuming all these equals that aren't.

We assume all kids are the same when it comes to strength, too. You know, we've seen the 12 year olds with the goatees and we've seen kids that were baby-faced.

But when it comes to the totals, the mistake we make is that we're taking the total based on the clicker or the chart. I always use this example. Let's say we go into the weight room and I give you two 30-pound dumbbells to curl. That's a pretty good curl, right? And I say, "Harold, do 15 and take seven to eight minutes off and then come back and we'll do another 15. Take seven, eight, nine minutes off and come back." You could go like that all day. All day. But if I say, "Harold, do 35 curls," you're going to hit muscle failure somewhere in the twenties, right? But then I say, "Take four or five minutes off and come back and do another 25."

Now let's start over.

Reynolds: Go ahead.

Reddick: So now we have the situation where you'll be in muscle failure. Right? So let's say we have a pitcher now who throws 15 pitches in the first inning, his team gets a runner on or maybe scores a run, goes back out and throws another 15, has a decent break and throws another 15. Do we have a problem with that kid continuing? No. That pitcher could throw seven innings at 15 pitches a clip, if he's efficient, and be fine. But the pitch count says we're going to pull him after a certain period of time. Now, the kid who goes into the first inning of the game and throws 35 pitches, that kid could be done right there.

He could be in muscle failure. Now, let's say his team goes down 1-2-3. Now he's back out there again, and maybe he throws 25 pitches. That kid has just thrown 50 to 55 pitches, and he is at far greater risk of injury and muscle failure and mechanical breakdown than the kid who has just thrown 105 pitches at a nice even pace.

Reynolds: Do you think though, Paul, we started off this whole thing with potential, and at the end of the day, when we got to potential it came down to parents scheduling all of these tournament games.

Reddick: Yep.

Reynolds: Do you think the pitch count is more parent-protective—"I've got to protect this player from his parent because this parent or coach will pitch him until he drops," more so than protecting the kid as an equal to his peers or compared to the others?

Reddick: Yeah. Unfortunately that's what it is. It's out there to protect the kids. But my argument is that we're not protecting them because it's not showing up anywhere. So are there going to be crazy parents? No matter what we do, we're not stopping crazy parents. But let's not let crazy parents stunt development. Let's not let our ability to educate the people in our league and our teams stop us from developing kids the right way.

When it comes to pitch counts—they haven't reduced injuries.

And I think it's stunting potential because kids aren't learning to be durable and to pitch. Now, in the big leagues, a five-inning start is like, "This guy went five innings. He really showed up for us today." It's a big deal. But like I said, we can't let the inmates run the asylum, so to speak.

Reynolds: You made a great point.

Reddick: I think that faction of baseball gets all of the attention. I think it's a lot smaller than we think. You know, I think it's a ...

Reynolds: It's a loud voice that's heard roaring in the desert.

Reddick: Right. Right.

Reynolds: It's louder than everybody else.

Reddick: If we go and we find any team right now and we look at the parents, it's going to be a break-up. You're going to have one parent that just doesn't care; his kid is just playing an activity. You're going to have one crazy, and everyone else is going to be in the middle. You know what I mean? They're going to be normal people.

Reynolds: So if I'm watching, I'm sitting at home and I'm thinking, "This crazy guy is shooting down Little League pitch counts and shooting down everything," then what's the answer, big shot?

Reddick: We need education. We need to be better informed and that's where it goes back to the bad information from credible sources. So if we're sitting in a room, with Little League baseball or me, who are we going to listen to? Now we're developing more of a voice.

We're the largest publisher of baseball information in the world and we're very proud of that, considering I started out of my grandmother's attic; which I was living in at the time. We've come a long way and we're doing our part and that's all anybody can do—just do their part and get information out like we're doing here.

But the biggest part with pitch counts—and we have a couple of teams studying this year—it's not how you get to them is important assuming angles line up and all that stuff. The biggest factor by far is how much time a player gets to rest between sets of pitches.

Let's go back to the weight room. And I say, "The reason you have trouble coming back to that set of 25 curls is because I didn't give you enough rest time." Right? When kids get into danger, it's because of the intervals. Now we can't control them all. But what we can control is that we can look for the early signs of injury. If we see a kid that throws 35 pitches in the first inning and the team goes down 1-2-3, there's things we can do to give him a little bit more rest. All right? We can take our time getting out there. We can talk to them. There's some things that we can do.

I'd argue that there should even be a little bit of time there, a minute or something there, to give them a little extra rest. That's probably too much. But that's where the problem happens. When this kid throws 35 pitches and he goes out in the second inning and he throws—he's probably done. We have to pull him.

So one of the educational things we have to do is recognize what the signs of injury are. Football's doing a great job with concussions now, right? They're identifying concussions earlier.

The first sign of injury in pitching is loss of control, when a pitcher loses control. All the guys you've known that have had surgery, Tommy John elbow surgery—and I stopped counting at something like 600 injured pitchers that I dealt with—if you ask them, they can trace that injury back to a day where they didn't feel right. You have to prod them a little bit. You've got to say, "Tommy, where did this start?" And they're like, "Ah, it just started hurting the other day." "No, no, no. When? Back it up." "Well, I had tendonitis last year." "Okay, go further.Was there a time when you lost control?" He goes, "Well, I was going good for a while and then I had a couple of bad games. I didn't know what was wrong. They rested me, I came back and I was okay and then I couldn't get it together." So there's a break—the first sign of injury is when something went wrong with the pitcher. There's somthing—the kid loses control.

And often, going back to the weight room, if you lift too much weight, if you get out too many times in those reps, what happens? Your form breaks down. So if we push you in those curls you're going to bend your knees, you're going to arch your back; you're going to get the weight up. Right? Well, a baseball's a weight. It's about five pounds for every 10 miles per hour. So an 80-mile-per-hour fastball is about 40 pounds of total pressure. So we're moving this weight. Now, if you're in the weight room and your form breaks down, trainers will yell at you across the gym, "Put that weight down. Your form broke down." You know, you're done. If your form breaks down, you're either lifting too heavy a weight or you went too many times.

We don't do that in pitching. We tell these kids, "See if you can finish the inning. See if we can pitch him through. How does he feel?" He feels fine. So now what do you tell a ten-year-old kid in a 32-team national tournament, pitching the championship game, when you ask, "How do you feel?" and he says, "I don't think I can go to-day." That's not going to happen. That kid's going to go. He's going to say, "I feel fine," because we've created this pressure, this situation to put them in, and kids push. And when you get into these tournament situations that's when pitch counts get out of control.

And we even see them on TV gaming it a little bit and saying, "Well, if he throws one more pitch he's got to take so many days off; so let's pull him so we can bring him back in two days and run that pitch count up again." It's a very interesting topic, but in everything we've done, there's been very little impact.

Reynolds: Very forward thinking. I hadn't heard the analogy tied to the weight room. That makes a lot of sense ...

Reddick: It's a weight, yeah.

Reynolds: ... when I hear that.

Reddick: Yeah.

Reynolds: And then the other thing is loss of control. Clearly, that's evident so people pay attention to it. I really like where you're headed with those things. I also like the suggestion, and you didn't say this so I'm going to take full credit for it, but you touched on it. But I really like the suggestion of a timer.

Reynolds: You threw 35 pitches; you've been sitting now for only one minute. You need to sit five minutes before you get to go back to the mound.

Reddick: Right.

Reynolds: You know what I mean?

Reddick: Yeah.

Reynolds: You've got a five-minute rally, guys, or else

he's done. You know, that type of thing.

Reddick: Right, but that goes back to the team. If you know your pitcher—if you're up and your first two hitters went down on the swing of the first pitch and you're the third guy, you can—that's education. You can slow that down.

Reynolds: Even if your league mandates it and says, "All right, all our games are going to be one hour and the pitchers are going to pitch such and such amount and there's got to be two minutes in between every inning so the pitcher can rest, to get back on the right track where he's rested." That's the whole forward thinking.

Reddick: Or if he reaches a pitch count. It should be at levels. So if he reaches an inordinate amount of pitches in one inning, something could kick in. Because I guarantee when we get these charts back at the end of this year, we're going to see that the pitchers that went out after—overall—now there's going to be some pitchers that are going to be on fire and they're going to roll, right, because that's the way athletics is. But I think we're going to see a real drop-off in productivity when there's that short rest. Because it's just endurance. It's just the way it goes.

So I think education is the way to go. I get so many emails about kids who are pitching both ends of a double header, and going back to our tournament discussion—could you imagine a time where Mariano Rivera would make a two-inning relief appearance? It's rare, right? It would be at the end of the season, the end of a championship series or something. Well, kids are doing this every weekend. That's kind of why we've had to put this clamp on these pitch counts. But a lot of these organizations that sponsor tournaments don't have pitch counts. They're kind of flying on their own. So Little League does, and I applaud them for the effort, but I think we need to get a little bit better.

Reynolds: Well, this has been very educational, very forward thinking, and very eye opening.

Reddick: All right.

Reynolds: So I appreciate it, bro.

Reddick: All right. Thanks, Harold. I appreciate it, man. Thank you.

48198833R00032

Made in the USA
Charleston, SC
26 October 2015